THE OFFICIAL
Newcastle United FC
ANNUAL 2012

Written by Mark Hannen

A Grange Publication

© 2011. Published by Grange Communications Ltd., Edinburgh under licence from Newcastle United Footbal Club.

Printed in the EU.

Every effort has been made to ensure the accuracy of information within this publication but the publishers cannot be held responsible for any errors or omissions. Views expressed are those of the author and do not necessarily represent those of the publishers or the football club. All rights reserved.

Photography © Ian Horrocks and Serena Taylor.

Thanks to Paul Joannou, Gavin Grieves, Amy Lockhart and Dan Sheridan.

ISBN: 978-1-908221-31-5

£7.99

It is my pleasure to welcome you to the 2012 Newcastle United Annual.

The 2010/11 season was a pretty good one for all supporters of the Club and one that all the players and staff enjoyed too.

The Premier League is as tough as it comes, especially for newly promoted teams, and I felt we acquitted ourselves extremely well and could so easily, with a little more luck, have finished a little higher than our eventual twelfth place finish. Everyone at the club pulled in the same direction and it was that togetherness, coupled with dedication, application, belief and ability that saw us maintain our Premier League status.

But that is all in the past and the 2011/12 season is all that concerns us. We enjoyed the summer, taking a short break from a frantic

season, but our aim now is to keep stabilising, developing, growing and improving this great football club.

I hope you enjoy reading this annual. It contains a tremendous range of information, the story of last season, the best goals we scored, profiles on all our first team players as well as great pieces of historical information that's great for young supporters to know about. Throw in many quizzes, competitions, a Premier League snakes and ladders game and much more besides, it all adds up to a thoroughly enjoyable read.

With very best wishes

**Alan Pardew
Team Manager**

Contents

a Season of Consolidation

After triumphantly winning the Championship in 2009/10, United's aim was to retain their place in the Premier League for the 2011/12 season. That they did in fine style with a 12th place finish, but without a few late goals along the way, and vital points slipping away, it could have been even better…

August

United were handed a daunting start to their Premier League campaign, a visit to Old Trafford to face a side who would go on to lift a record number of top flight titles come the end of the season. Newcastle gave a good account of themselves and could have led early on. The final 3 – 0 scoreline was perhaps a little harsh on the Magpies but their performance gave them plenty of hope going into the first home game of the season – a fixture against managerless Aston Villa. What a day that turned out to be as United hit six without reply past the hapless Villans with Andy Carroll netting three goals in the gorgeous late summer sunshine. Things may

United celebrate Barton's opener against Villa

Hatem Ben Arfa is congratulated after his winner at Goodison Park

not have gone so well though, had John Carew not blazed an early penalty way over the Gallowgate End crossbar. The month ended with a trip to Molineux, to face a Wolves side who were to prove a match for the very best on their home patch during the course of the season. Andy Carroll proved to be 'johnny on the spot' once more heading in a second half equalizer to earn United a more than deserved share of the spoils.

Pl	W	D	L	F	A	Pts	Pos
3	1	1	1	7	4	4	8

September

After a weekend of International football, Premier League new-boys Blackpool were the next visitors to Tyneside with the home side confident of building on a good start to the season. Alas, it was not to

be for Chris Hughton's side, as two goals from the visitors, right at the end of each half, condemned the Magpies, who had Frenchman Hatem Ben Arfa making his debut, to their first home league defeat since May 2009. Thankfully, the pain of defeat was only short-lived, as United bounced back in fine style with a single goal victory at Everton, Goodison Park witnessing a superb maiden strike by Ben Arfa. A shock, but nevertheless fully merited Carling Cup win at Chelsea followed, but the month ended in great disappointment as United succumbed to a second bitterly disappointing home defeat, this time against Stoke City. United had led at the break, and for the only time during the whole season, went on to lose a game after going into the dressing room after 45 minutes with their noses in front.

Pl	W	D	L	F	A	Pts	Pos
6	2	1	3	9	8	7	10

Shola Ameobi nets from the spot to make it 3 for United

October

United were unlucky to lose at Manchester City against their big-spending hosts in a game that, sadly, would be remembered for Nigel de Jong's tackle, which broke Ben Arfa's leg and ultimately, brought a premature end to the Frenchman's season. The following week United were indebted to an injury time equaliser from Fabricio Coloccini to salvage a point against Wigan whilst seven days later, Kevin Nolan and Andy Carroll scored the goals at Upton Park, which kept up the Magpies' fine away form. United were bundled out of the Carling Cup by a fine Arsenal side but the month was rounded off in unbelievable style with a five-star performance against local rivals Sunderland. Incredibly, United were three up at the break, two goals from skipper Kevin Nolan and a penalty from Shola Ameobi. Both players found the net again in the

second half, the former completing a dream derby-day hat-trick to wrap up a win that sent the Geordie masses home in unbridled euphoria.

Pl	W	D	L	F	A	Pts	Pos
10	4	2	4	19	14	14	7

November

United travelled to the Emirates brimming with confidence and that was proven to be well founded as an Andy Carroll header, and some fine goalkeeping from Tim Krul, earned the visitors a tremendous victory, their first at Arsenal's new home. Two home games followed with Newcastle looking

for a six-point haul however, the football fates, the ones that pour cold water over enthusiastic and hopeful fans, conspired to bring only one point into the Magpies' nest as Blackburn snatched all three and Fulham ground out a goalless draw. Catastrophe followed at the Reebok Stadium in the next game, with United on the end of a 5 – 1 drubbing and in many ways, being the architects of their own downfall. A good point against Premier League Champions Chelsea rounded off the month, Andy Carroll seizing on an early error in the Londoners defence, which gifted the Magpies the lead, but a deflected effort from Saloman Kalou on the stroke of half time levelled things up.

Pl	W	D	L	F	A	Pts	Pos
15	5	4	6	23	22	19	9

December

Newcastle were never in the game at The Hawthorns as the Baggies ran out comfortable 3 – 1 winners, United's consolation goal coming in the dying embers of the game. It was after that defeat that the Board decided to part company with manager Chris Hughton and bring in former Reading, West Ham, Charlton and Southampton boss Alan Pardew. And what a start the new man had as he watched his new charges take on and emphatically beat Liverpool 3 – 1 under the floodlights at St. James' Park in great style. Heavy snow forced the postponement of United's fixture in Birmingham the following week. Meanwhile, two defeats, at the hands of Manchester City at home and Tottenham at White Hart Lane, brought a disappointing end to what had been a pretty good year, which included winning the Championship and performing admirably in the first season back in the Premier League.

Pl	W	D	L	F	A	Pts	Pos
19	6	4	9	28	31	22	13

Andy Caroll heads the winner against Arsenal

It's a hat-trick for Leon Best

January

The New Year kicked off in the best possible way. Six points and two clean sheets from games at Wigan and at home to West Ham, the latter seeing a five goal demolition of the Hammers at St. James' Park, Leon Best marking his first Premier League start with a hat-trick, United's third of the season following in the footsteps of Kevin Nolan and Andy Carroll. United's FA Cup hopes were quickly extinguished at Stevenage before the Magpies returned to league action across the water at the Stadium of Light. The home side were desperate for revenge but it was United who dominated throughout and only an injury time goal from Asamoah Gyan, which wiped out Kevin Nolan's earlier strike, prevented the Geordies from being able to celebrate a double over

their Wearside neighbours. A week later and Newcastle were once again 'robbed' of all three points late on, this time Aaron Lennon grabbing a last minute leveller for Tottenham at St. James' Park, cancelling out Fabricio Coloccini's opener.

Pl	W	D	L	F	A	Pts	Pos
23	8	6	9	36	33	30	8

February

A busy month kicked off with defeat at Fulham. United were without Andy Carroll, who had been sold to Liverpool for £35m on transfer deadline day, and in the early stages of the game they lost Shola Ameobi too, after a clash with Steve Sidwell left the popular forward with a broken cheekbone. Three days later it got worse, a whole lot worse, as United found themselves four down to Arsenal after the first 45 minutes of a nightmare half at St. James' Park. What followed though, went down in Premier League history as United stormed back to level the game with Cheik Tiote's late volley arrowing past Wojciech Szczesny to bring the house down at Gallowgate. The next three games against the B's of Blackburn, Birmingham and Bolton brought two draws and a win which proved a decent return of points given two of the games were away from home. The performance at St Andrews was particularly praiseworthy, as was the home draw with Bolton, given United played much of the game with only 10-men after the dismissal of Ryan Taylor.

Pl	W	D	L	F	A	Pts	Pos
28	9	9	10	43	39	36	9

March

An international break and the playing of the FA Cup Sixth Round ties meant that Newcastle, after playing five games in the last 24 days would now, bizarrely, have only two games in the next 35! And it was to be a no point March for United too, with defeats against Everton and Stoke giving Spring a depressing start on Tyneside at least. Leon Best netted against the Toffees, his sixth goal in nine outings, but goals from Leon Osman and Phil Jagielka gave the Merseysiders a deserved victory against a below-par United. Stoke City, who were marching to Wembley in the FA Cup, overran Newcastle at the Britannia and ended up 4 – 0 winners. Defensive errors contributed to a bad away for Alan Pardew's men who were left to pick themselves up off the floor, dust themselves down and prepare for a series of vital fixtures in April – games that would secure United's place in the Premier League for the 2011/12 season.

Pl	W	D	L	F	A	Pts	Pos
30	9	9	12	44	45	36	11

Tim Howard is beaten by Leon Best but Toffees triumph

Shola Ameobi nets against Wolves

April

Defeat to Wolves on the first Saturday of April would have dragged United into a dreaded relegation battle. Thankfully those thoughts, if they had indeed ever entered the minds of the staff and players, were banished inside the first 50 minutes when United romped into a three-goal lead, eventually running out easy 4 – 1 victors. A single goal loss at Aston Villa followed before United took on Champions elect, Manchester United, at St. James' Park. There were no goals on a fiery passionate Tyneside night but it was a nil-nil draw enjoyed by all of those present

at Gallowgate. An equally, if not more important point, was secured at Bloomfield Road the following weekend which kept the home side in the relegation mire, a fight they were ultimately set to lose on the season's dramatic final Sunday afternoon.

Pl	W	D	L	F	A	Pts	Pos
34	10	11	13	49	48	41	9

May

With Andy Carroll appearing as a second half substitute for Liverpool, the Reds ran out comfortable three goal winners against United at Anfield. The Magpies put that behind them though and in beating Birmingham City at St. James' Park in their next game, they secured their Premier League status, a just reward for their efforts during the course of the season. Liam Ridgewell saw red for the visitors, which undoubtedly aided United's cause and would prove very costly to the Blues come the end of the season. A fine 2 – 2 draw at Chelsea came next, Steven Taylor heading a deserved injury time equalizer for United before Newcastle saw out the season with another draw, this time a six-goal topsy-turvy encounter against West Brom. United were three up just after the interval and in sloppily throwing away their advantage, they also slipped from a possible ninth place finish to their eventual twelfth place finish in a matter of minutes as the curtain came down on another great season of Premier League football.

Pl	W	D	L	F	A	Pts	Pos
38	11	13	14	56	57	46	12

A joyous Steven Taylor after his late leveller at Stamford Bridge

	League	FA Cup	Lge Cup	2010/11	Total NUFC
Phil AIREY	0 (0) 0	0 (1) 0	0 (0) 0	0 (0) 0	0 (1) 0
Sammy AMEOBI	0 (1) 0	0 (0) 0	0 (0) 0	0 (0) 0	0 (1) 0
Shola AMEOBI	21 (7) 6	0 (0) 0	2 (0) 3	23 (7) 9	184 (119) 70
Joey BARTON	32 (0) 4	1 (0) 1	0 (2) 0	33 (2) 5	67 (15) 8
Hatem BEN ARFA	3 (1) 1	0 (0) 0	0 (0) 0	3 (1) 1	3 (1) 1
Leon BEST	9 (2) 6	1 (0) 0	0 (0) 0	10 (2) 6	16 (9) 6
Sol CAMPBELL	4 (3) 0	0 (0) 0	1 (0) 0	5 (3) 0	5 (3) 0
Andy CARROLL	18 (1) 11	0 (0) 0	0 (1) 0	18 (2) 11	60 (31) 33
Fabricio COLOCCINI	35 (0) 2	1 (0) 0	1 (0) 0	37 (0) 2	115 (0) 4
Ryan DONALDSON	0 (0) 0	0 (0) 0	1 (0) 0	1 (0) 0	2 (4) 0
Jose ENRIQUE	36 (0) 0	0 (0) 0	0 (0) 0	36 (0) 0	121 (8) 1
Shane FERGUSON	3 (4) 0	0 (0) 0	2 (0) 0	5 (4) 0	5 (4) 0
Dan GOSLING	0 (1) 0	0 (0) 0	0 (0) 0	0 (0) 0	0 (1) 0
Danny GUTHRIE	11 (3) 0	0 (0) 0	1 (0) 0	12 (3) 0	76 (9) 7
Jonas GUTIERREZ	34 (3) 3	0 (0) 0	1 (1) 0	35 (4) 3	96 (17) 7
Steve HARPER	18 (0) 0	0 (0) 0	0 (0) 0	18 (0) 0	180 (10) 0
Stephen IRELAND	0 (2) 0	0 (0) 0	0 (0) 0	0 (2) 0	0 (2) 0
Tamas KADAR	0 (0) 0	0 (0) 0	2 (0) 0	2 (0) 0	11 (7) 0
Tim KRUL	20 (1) 0	1 (0) 0	3 (0) 0	24 (1) 0	31 (3) 0
Shefki KUQI	0 (6) 0	0 (0) 0	0 (0) 0	0 (6) 0	0 (6) 0
Peter LOVENKRANDS	18 (7) 6	1 (0) 0	3 (0) 1	22 (7) 7	51 (22) 26
Kazenga LUALUA	0 (2) 0	0 (0) 0	1 (0) 0	1 (2) 0	3 (12) 0
Kevin NOLAN	30 (0) 12	1 (0) 0	0 (1) 0	31 (1) 12	88 (3) 30
James PERCH	9 (4) 0	1 (0) 0	1 (0) 0	11 (4) 0	11 (4) 0
Nile RANGER	1 (23) 0	0 (1) 0	3 (0) 1	4 (24) 1	11 (47) 3
Wayne ROUTLEDGE	10 (7) 0	1 (0) 0	1 (0) 0	12 (7) 0	27 (9) 3
Danny SIMPSON	30 (0) 0	1 (0) 0	0 (0) 0	31 (0) 0	72 (0) 1
Alan SMITH	7 (4) 0	1 (0) 0	2 (0) 0	10 (4) 0	77 (15) 0
James TAVERNIER	0 (0) 0	0 (0) 0	1 (0) 0	1 (0) 0	2 (0) 0
Ryan TAYLOR	3 (2) 0	0 (0) 0	3 (0) 2	6 (2) 2	38 (16) 6
Steven TAYLOR	12 (2) 3	0 (0) 0	0 (0) 0	12 (2) 3	174 (13) 13
Cheil TIOTE	26 (0) 1	0 (1) 0	0 (1) 0	26 (2) 1	26 (2) 1
Haris VUCKIC	0 (0) 0	0 (0) 0	3 (0) 0	3 (0) 0	4 (3) 0
XISCO	0 (2) 0	0 (0) 0	0 (0) 0	0 (2) 0	4 (7) 1
Mike WILLIAMSON	28 (1) 0	1 (0) 0	1 (1) 0	30 (2) 0	46 (2) 0

In addition, the following players made the matchday 18 but
never got off the bench: **Michael Richardson** and **Ole Soderberg**

Classic Clashes

Newcastle United have been involved in many memorable and outstanding matches in their history. Some are labelled 'great' because of the excitement generated, some by their significance and some by the terrific football played and quality of the goals scored.

Games such as the 5-0 hammering of Manchester United in 1996 and the 3-2 defeat of Barcelona in 1997 will always be high on the list, hence their inclusion in the 2011 Annual, but we can't let events of last season go unreported so here we relive two marvellous St. James' Park occasions, the visits of Sunderland and Arsenal to Tyneside.

Both games wil be remembered for years to come; the fantastic football, the goals in each game and the unique crackling atmosphere the Geordie supporters generated inside a vibrant, heaving and ear-shattering St. James' Park.

October 31st 2010
Premier League
Newcastle United 5 Sunderland 1

In one of the most memorable Tyne-Wear derbies in recent memory, a Kevin Nolan hat-trick and a Shola Ameobi double gave Newcastle United a thumping 5-1 win over Sunderland.

Nolan became the first Magpies player since Peter Beardsley in 1985 to take home the matchball in a game against The Black Cats, while Ameobi continued his remarkable recent scoring record against the Wearsiders – a day of jubilation for the black and whites.

There was certainly plenty of passion inside St. James' in a fast and furious opening, Andy Carroll burst through in the 12th minute and was only denied a clear run on goal by a great last-ditch tackle from Phil Bardsley before a Joey Barton corner was met by Carroll. Belgian keeper Simon Mignolet made a good save but Fabricio Coloccini dived to meet the rebound – only for his header to hit Ameobi and go wide.

Mignolet made another save to deny Barton from 20 yards – but from the resulting corner, The Magpies went 1-0 up thanks to a wonderful piece of improvisation from captain Kevin Nolan. He was virtually lying flat on his back as Barton's flag-kick came to him but he produced a powerful overhead kick before being piled upon by his team-mates.

Nolan then saw a 20-yard effort zip just wide, with the Sunderland keeper scrambling across his goal, but soon got his second. The ball was played into the area and Carroll went for a bicycle kick; he didn't get the connection he wanted, but it fell kindly for the unmarked Nolan who controlled the ball and finished easily.

On the stroke of half time, referee Dowd awarded United a penalty, Gutierrez was brought down as he surged into the box and Shola Ameobi – who scored with such aplomb from the spot in this fixture two seasons ago – stepped up to convert from 12 yards to give Newcastle a 3-0 advantage at the break.

Bramble saw red for a late tackle on Gutierrez before United made it four on 70 minutes. Simpson played another great ball in and Carroll rose to meet it, only for his header to cannon back off the crossbar. Ameobi, though, was following in and although he still had plenty to do, he smashed a half-volley into the net from 12 yards for his fourth goal in three outings against the Wearsiders.

Then came the fifth - and Nolan's third. Barton, whose delivery all day was exceptional, took a corner after his free-kick had been deflected behind, and Ameobi won it before Nolan diverted it home to grab the second hat-trick of his United career, 13 months after his other treble at Ipswich Town in September 2009.

Bent pulled one back in stoppage time but it was far too late to change the outcome and Newcastle recorded a famous derby victory – what a game!

United Krul, Simpson, Enrique, Coloccini, Williamson, Barton, Tiote, Nolan, Gutierrez, Carroll, Ameobi (Ranger 86)

Goals
Newcastle
Nolan 26, 34, 75, Ameobi 45 pen, 70

Sunderland
Bent 90

Attendance 51,988

A stunning second half comeback saw Newcastle recover from four down at half-time to draw 4-4 against Arsenal at St. James' Park.

Arsenal got off to a dream start in just 43 seconds. Joey Barton's sliding tackle in the middle of the park saw the ball run into the path of Theo Walcott, who raced in behind Fabricio Coloccini and slipped the ball past Steve Harper.

And if that was good, then it got even better for Arsenal in the third minute as Newcastle were left facing a mountain to climb so early on. Andrei Arshavin swung in a free-kick from the left flank and Johan Djourou nipped in ahead of Mike Williamson to send a free header into the top corner.

But a bad afternoon just got worse in the 10th minute when the Gunners made it 3-0. Abou Diaby fed Walcott down the right and his low centre was comfortably swept home by Robin Van Persie.

And number four duly arrived on 26 minutes, and again stemmed from a flowing Arsenal move down the right. Diaby played in full-back

Kevin Nolan is buried after his opener in the derby

Joey Barton calmly watches his penalty hit the back of the net

Bacary Sagna, whose cross was inch-perfect for Van Persie to steal in unmarked and head home from close range.

Newcastle were given the faintest glimmer of hope five minutes after the restart when the Gunners were reduced to 10 men, Diaby seeing red after a tangle with Barton.

The hosts reduced the deficit on 69 minutes through Barton's fourth goal of the season. As the midfielder drilled a low corner in towards Best, he was bundled over by Koscielny. Barton stepped up to confidently roll the penalty into the bottom left corner, sending Szczesny the wrong way.

It was constant Newcastle pressure now. Leon Best had a goal ruled out for offside, but the big front man was not to be denied again and Best made it 4-2 in the 75th minute, reacting quickest to a loose ball in the area and thumping a shot home from close range.

The comeback became a real possibility with just six minutes of the match remaining, thanks to another spot kick. Koscielny was again the guilty culprit, fouling Williamson, and Barton kept his cool to drill the penalty straight down the middle and just past the legs of the diving Szczesny.

United
Harper, Simpson, Enrique, Coloccini, Williamson, Barton, Tiote, Nolan, Gutierrez, Best (Guthrie 90), Lovenkrands (Ranger 73)

Goals
Newcastle
(Barton 69pen, 84pen; Best 75; Tiote 88)
Arsenal
(Walcott 1; Djourou 3; Van Persie 10, 26)

Attendance 51,561

Amazingly, the turnaround was completed in the 88th minute – and through one of the goals of the season. Cheik Tiote smashed home his first in the black and white striped shirt, thumping a 30-yard volley past the helpless Szczesny as Arsenal headed clear a corner.

Kevin Nolan almost won it, sending a strike just wide of the upright with Szczesny beaten, but the Geordies had to settle for a draw which, 45 minutes earlier, looked impossible to salvage.

United's Premier League Goalkeepers

It's said you have to be 'mad' to be a goalkeeper. They are indeed a special breed, but they are the ones who stop the goals and win you the points, assuming their teammates put the ball in the net at the other end of course! In this annual we're looking at all the goalkeepers, stoppers, custodians or whatever you want to call them, who have kept goal for United in the Premier League era.

United are about to enter their 18th season of Premier League football and in that time, eight men have stood between the sticks for United, and a further four have got on to the bench without ever being called upon.

Strangely enough, from 1993-1999, seven of those eight made their league debuts for United in a six-year period, with the eighth, Tim Krul, not getting the call until 2010, a full 11 years later!

Taking things from the start, a home game with Tottenham Hotspur in August 1993 saw **Pavel Srnicek** take to the field in an opening day 1-0 defeat against the Londoners. Pavel had a shaky start at United but blossomed into a top drawer keeper and a fan favourite. The popular Czech was unconventional at times and, of all the keepers listed, whilst possibly not being the most consistent, was capable of pulling off the most sensational of acrobatic stops.

Irishman **Tommy Wright** was next in line. Having played in Division Two for United (what is now termed the Championship) the burly stopper enjoyed a successful but short period on Tyneside. Leaving in 1993 he returned briefly in 1999 and was unfortunate enough to play in the 2-1 home defeat to Sunderland,

the game better remembered for the monsoon conditions, and of course Ruud Gullit leaving Alan Shearer and Duncan Ferguson on the substitutes bench.

Mike Hooper was signed from Liverpool with the intention of installing him as United's No 1 but his time at Gallowgate didn't turn out as he and the club hoped and he was relegated to third choice behind Srnicek and Shaka Hislop, only playing 30 times for the black'n'whites.

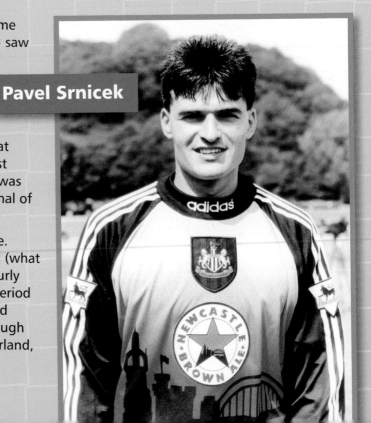

Pavel Srnicek

Shaka Hislop

John Karelese had a very brief spell between the sticks, only three game infact, letting in seven goals in the process, but the amiable Dutchman was never really more than back up to Shay and Steve and that always counted against him.

The most recent incumbent of the goalkeeper shirt is Dutch international **Tim Krul.** Tim, who made his full international debut in June 2011 against the mighty Brazil, and kept a clean sheet too, actually made his debut in the UEFA Cup back in 2006 as an 18-year old but only stepped up to the Premier League last season when he came on as a substitute for Steve Harper at Everton, going on to make a further 20 starts throughout the rest of the season.

And there are four unlucky lads, players who have been in the matchday squad but who never got the call from the bench. Three of those players, Lionel Perez, John Burridge and Tony Caig, will never get their chance, but Swedish youngster Ole Soderberg, who was on the bench 19 times last season, may well get his opportunity in the future. It is worth noting that Burridge did play for United on 84 occasions in the days before the Premier League started.

London born but Trinidadian, raised **Shaka Hislop** (his first name originates from that of a Zulu king) debuted in 1995 and was a huge presence between the posts. He'd starred for Reading before joining United and was a 'safe pair of hands' and, with his height (6'4") very dominant in the air too.

Now with over 100 caps for the Republic of Ireland (81 of which were won whilst he was at St. James' Park, a club record) **Shay Given** was heading for United's all-time appearance record before leaving in 2009 for Manchester City. Widely recognised as one of the top keepers in the Premier League, Shay was a fixture in United's line up through most of the 2000s and deservedly goes down as one of United's finest of all time.

Next up for United, making his debut in November 1998, is **Steve Harper,** who is of course currently the longest serving player on United's books. Steve played in the 1999 FA Cup Final at Wembley in only his 10th appearance for the club. Sadly the Magpies lost 2-0 that afternoon. Loyalty and Steve Harper go together like socks and shoes but Steve was and still is much more than that, a true top class keeper who was very unfortunate not to gain any international recognition.

Steve Harper

As little as 25 years ago, virtually every goalkeeper up and down the country would don a plain green top and wear the number one on their shirt – how times have changed. Shirts are now virtually every colour under the sun and the squad numbering system means the famous no 1 shirt is not always the choice of those who stand between the posts.

And if you're looking for some stand out saves, how about Shay Given's stunning effort to thwart Kevin Phillips at the Stadium of Light in 2002, Tim Krul's superb reactions to turn away Samir Nasri's strike at the Emirates or Steve Harper's one man show in keeping the Blades at bay at Bramall Lane during the Championship winning season.

Summary

in order of their first appearance for United in the Premier League

Pavel Srnicek	1990 – 98 and 2006 190 appearances
Shaka Hislop	1995 – 98 71 appearances
Mike Hooper	1993 – 96 30 appearances
Shay Given	1997 – 2009 463 appearances
Steve Harper	1998 – date 190 appearances
Tommy Wright	1988 – 93 and 1999 87 appearances
John Karelse	1999 – 2003 3 appearances
Tim Krul	2006 – date 34 appearances

Shay Given

United's Premier League Goalkeepers

Newcastle United
Premier League Snakes and Ladders

70	69	68. Red Card v Sunderland.	67	66	65. Late for training, go back 4 spaces.	64
57	58	59	60	61	62	63. Concede penalty, go back 4 spaces.
56	55	54. Head crucial late winner, advance 5 spaces.	53	52	51. Booked.	50
43	44	45. Hit superb hat-trick.	46	47	48	49
42. Injured.	41. Goal line clearance.	40. Heavy defeat, go back 5 spaces.	39	38	37	36
29	30	31	32	33	34. Great header.	35
28. Sign boot deal, advance 3 spaces.	27	26	25	24	23	22
15	16	17	18. Club fine. Go back to square 9.	19	20	21
14. New club car, advance 3 spaces.	13	12	11	10. Beat Sunderland 5-1.	9	8
	2	3	4. Named club captain.	5	6	7. Own goal horror go back to start.

FA Cup & League Cup Reviews

Gunners End Carling Cup Dream

Rd 2: Accrington Stanley 2 3 Newcastle United

Rd 3: Chelsea 3 4 Newcastle United

Rd 4: Newcastle United 0 4 Arsenal

United's record in the League Cup is, to put it mildly, not the best. One solitary Final appearance (back in 1976) in the 50-year history of the competition isn't a lot to crow about – sadly 2010/11 was to be no different, even though hopes were high after a terrific Third Round win at Stamford Bridge.

The road to Wembley began at the Crown Ground, home of Accrington Stanley. In front of a live TV audience, sensing an upset no doubt, United ran out comfortable winners even though there was only one goal in it at the end of the 90 minutes.

Ryan Taylor crashed in a superb 30-yarder to give United the lead but sloppy defending

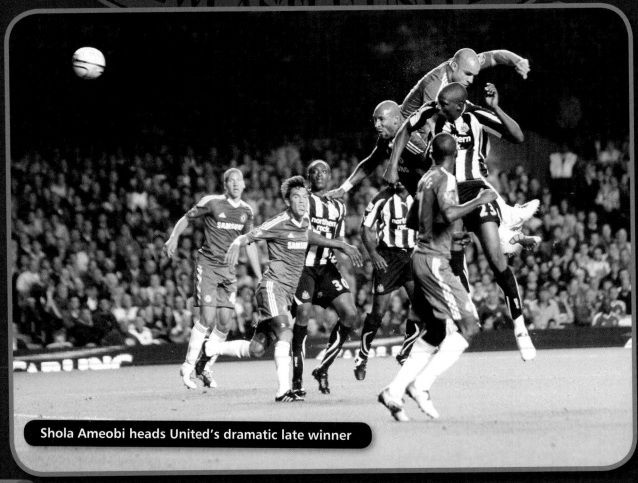

Shola Ameobi heads United's dramatic late winner

gave Ray Putterill the chance to level on the stroke of half time. In the second half Shola Ameobi and Peter Lovenkrands put the game beyond Stanley, Sean Hessey's injury time strike proving nothing more than a consolation.

Chelsea away in Round Three wasn't what the Doctor ordered but United put in a fabulous show to record their first win at the Bridge since 1986.

Shola Ameobi headed a dramatic 90th minute winner for United in front of their delirious fans after goals from Van Aanholt and Anelka (2) were matched by strikes from Ryan Taylor, Ranger and Ameobi, which had left the game tied at 3 – 3 and the probability of extra-time.

So after disposing of Chelsea, another London 'giant' were next out of the hat for United in Arsenal, but this time the Magpies had home advantage. Not that it helped though. An even first half saw Arsenal snatch the lead on 45 minutes via a Tim Krul own goal before second half goals from Walcott (2) and Bendtner sealed an emphatic win for the eventual runners-up in the competition.

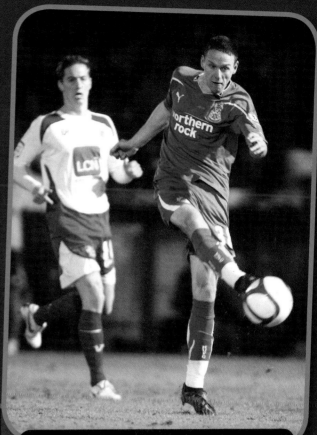
Phil Airey in debut action at Stevenage

Stevenage Get Their Revenge On United

Rd 3: Stevenage 3 1 Newcastle United

The FA Cup remains a magical competition, no more so than for fans of Newcastle United, and once again, come the first week of January, hopes were high that this was to be 'our' year'.

Stevenage away in Round Three looked a decent draw on paper but it was the home side that deservedly triumphed, avenging their defeat to the Magpies back in 1998.

The ESPN cameras were present as a capacity crowd packed into the Lamex Stadium on Broadhall Way, the home fans full of anticipation and sensing blood – and that's exactly what they got.

The home side completely bossed the first half and it was a fortunate United who trooped off at the interval with the scoresheet still blank. But five minutes after the break, a Stacy Long shot from 25 yards took a huge deflection off Mike Williamson giving keeper Tim Krul absolutely no chance as the ball diverted past him.

And five minutes later, before the cheers had subsided, and the red and whites riding the crest of a wave, they made it two. Three sides of the ground erupted as Michael Bostwick strode forward, unchallenged, to strike a powerful shot past Krul via the post.

Substitute Cheik Tiote was red-carded soon after coming on as a substitute as United struggled to get a foot-hold in the game. Joey Barton rifled in a corker from 30 yards in injury time but whatever faint hope United had of getting a replay was immediately dashed as almost straight from the re-start Peter Winn sealed the tie for Stevenage – and how they celebrated on the final whistle – both players and fans.

United were left to lick their wounds and move on, which is exactly what they did, by travelling to the Stadium of Light and putting on a great performance on Wearside.

TOP 10 GOALSCORERS

In previous annuals, we've looked at the all time greats that have lined up for the Magpies over the years. This time we're focussing purely on the top 10 goalscorers in United's history, starting from the top

Alan Shearer

(1996-2006) – 206 goals

Scorer of a record 206 goals for the Magpies, Shearer is the archetypal Geordie Hero. Joining United from Blackburn after Euro 96 for a world record £15m, Shearer fulfilled his boyhood dream by pulling on the black and white United shirt and banging in goal after goal at the Gallowgate and Leazes Ends. A two-time FA Cup finalist in 1998 and 1999, Alan's career at Newcastle was hampered by a number of serious injuries but that didn't stop him becoming probably the most legendary name in United's illustrious history.

Jackie Milburn

(1943-1957) – 200 goals

Wor Jackie held Newcastle United's goalscoring record until 2006 when Alan Shearer surpassed his tremendous feat. Born in Ashington, local boy Jackie became a St James' Park hero as his goalscoring ability took Tyneside by storm. Widely recognised as one of the best in the business, he scored many breathtaking goals. Jackie relished the big match atmosphere and created headlines over and over again with his spectacular strikes. A three time FA Cup winner with the Magpies in the 1950s, Jackie began life as a pit apprentice before football became a way of life for him. With 13 caps for England, Jackie left an impression on everyone who saw him play, or knew him as a person.

Len White

(1953-1962) – 153 goals

Len White took over the United goalscoring mantle from Jackie Milburn and Vic Keeble in the late 1950s and only Wor Jackie and Alan Shearer have scored more goals for the Magpies in league and cup football. A Yorkshireman, Len was of stocky build but possessed terrific strength on the ball, weaving in and out of challenges at speed and finishing with a power-packed shot. He loved to attack defences on his own and would set the Gallowgate crowd roaring with many a spectacular goal. Unfortunate not to win a full England cap, Len did notch a notable eight minute hat-trick playing for a Football League XI against Ireland.

Hughie Gallacher

(1925-1930) – 143 goals

'Wee Hughie', as he was affectionately known, was perhaps one of the greatest centre-forwards ever to pull on a Newcastle shirt, and at just 5ft 5", what he lacked in height he made up for in goals – and plenty of them. A tenacious striker, Gallacher's United record is as impressive as any, with the Scot lashing an unbelievable 143 goals in just 160 appearances, including 39 in 41 during the 1926/27 season, where he also skippered the side to League title glory.

Malcolm Macdonald

(1971–76) – 121 goals

A seventies icon, Supermac, as he was nicknamed on Tyneside, was hero worshipped at St. James' Park for his goal scoring feats and the excitement he brought to the United supporters. Built like a middle-weight boxer, he was a brash and colourful centre-forward. Blessed with electric pace and a thunderous shot, Supermac terrorised defences up and down the country scoring 121 goals for United in only 258 appearances. A hat-trick against Liverpool on his home debut signalled his intention and he also hit five goals in an England shirt against Cyprus in 1975. Malcolm was a huge personality in the region and firmly cemented his place as one of our Number 9 heroes.

Peter Beardsley

(1983-87 & 1993–97) – 119 goals

A true United legend, Peter appeared for the Magpies in two separate spells, first with the likes of Kevin Keegan and Chris Waddle in the mid 1980s, and then under Keegan the Manager, 10 years on when the Magpies took the Premiership by storm. Peter is recognised by many as the best player to have pulled on the black and white shirt, slight of build but possessing fantastic ball skills and marvellous vision. The holder of 59 England caps, Peter scored 119 goals in 326 appearances for United, many of which were truly spectacular – the end product of splendid placement, precision timing or delightful dribbles.

Neil Harris

(1920-1925) – 101 goals

A dashing striker, Harris had a great eye for goal and possessed a stinging shot. Small at only 5'7", he was speedy and a prolific goalscorer and only one of nine players to score over 100 goals for the Magpies. He found a rich vein of form as United headed for FA Cup success in 1924, scoring in the Final. Capped by Scotland too, he went on to manage Swansea and Swindon. He was from a footballing family – his brother was a noted player as well whilst his son John appeared with distinction for Chelsea.

Bobby Mitchell

(1949-1961) – 113 goals

Along with club colleagues Frank Brennan and Jackie Milburn, Bobby Mitchell was the darling of the Newcastle crowd during the immediate post war years. Known throughout football as 'Bobby Dazzler' he was famed for his immaculate ball control and wing wizardry and scored many an important goal for United, especially in FA Cup ties. A three time Cup winner, Bobby thrilled the United crowd with his magic footwork and ball skills in a 13-year Gallowgate career that saw him hit the net 113 times in 410 appearances. Brought up in the shadows of Hampden Park in Glasgow, Bobby also scored on his debut for Scotland.

Bryan 'Pop' Robson

(1962-71) – 97 goals

A junior product at United who turned into a potent striker. Scoring on his debut at Charlton, 'Pop' as he was affectionately known, was sharp, quick on the turn, and teamed up superbly with fellow striker, big Wyn Davies. Very unlucky not to win an England cap, 'Pop' was a key figure in United's Fairs Cup triumph in 1969, scoring 6 times during the campaign. A scorer of many long range spectacular goals, he also served West Ham and Sunderland with distinction.

Tom McDonald

(1921-1931) – 113 goals

From Inverness in the Highlands of Scotland, Tom was one of United's key players as they lifted the FA Cup in 1924, and the League Championship in 1927. An unsung hero, he was an attacking inside forward who also netted over a century of goals for the Magpies. A real team man, he worked hard in the midfield and linked superbly with Hughie Gallacher and Stan Seymour. After his retirement he served United as a club steward, looking after the press box high up in the old West Stand.

TOP 10 GOALSCORERS

season quiz 2010/11

What do you remember about the 2010/11 season?

1 Who scored United's last goal of 2010 and first of 2011?

2 Who knocked United out of the FA Cup?

3 Who scored United's first hat-trick of the season?

4 Which team did United sign Cheik Tiote from?

5 Which team did United play competitively for the first time last season?

6 Which two teams did Newcastle fail to score against last season?

7 Which two teams did United do the 'double' over last season?

8 At the end of the season, Tim Krul made his international debut against which team?

9 How many penalties did Shola Ameobi score last season?

10 Against which team did United record their highest attendance in 2010/11?

Answers on page 60

Player Profiles

MEHDI ABEID

Born	6 August 1992, Montreuil, France
Debut	—
Previous Club	Lens
Appearances/Goals	0/0

Mehdi arrived on Tyneside from Lens on 1 July 2011 signing a five-year deal after impressing whilst on trial at the end of the 2010/11 season. He has represented France at Under 17 and Under 18 level and is a right footed attacking midfielder who can also play in a forward position. Of French/Algerian descent, Mehdi may well be one for the future but aims to make an impact at St. James' Park as soon as he can.

SHOLA AMEOBI

Born	12 October 1981, Zaria, Nigeria
Debut	9 September 2000 v Chelsea (H)
Previous Club	Academy
Appearances/Goals	303/70

Fired in 9 goals for United last season, including two more against Sunderland, taking his tally against United's deadliest rivals to six. A talented striker with a penchant for the unpredictable, Shola was born in Nigeria and came to England with his parents at the age of five. A product of the Academy, he is United's all-time leading European scorer with 12 goals. Shola has passed the 300-game mark for the Magpies and should have a key role to play once more in 2011/12.

SAMMY AMEOBI

Born	1 May 1992, Newcastle
Debut	15 May 2011 v Chelsea (A)
Previous Club	Academy
Appearances/Goals	1/0

Sammy, younger brother of fellow United striker Shola, broke into the first team at the end of last season and impressed in the 2011/12 pre season games. Like Shola, he is hugely talented and packs a cracking shot, particularly on his left side. Co-incidentally made his debut against the same opposition (Chelsea) as Shola, over a decade apart, but was delighted to be alongside his brother at Stamford Bridge last season. Sammy has also represented Nigeria at youth level.

All statistics current to beginning of 2011/12 season

DEMBA BA

Born	23 May 1985, Paris
Debut	—
Previous Club	West Ham
Appearances/Goals	0/0

Senegal international striker Demba Ba joined Newcastle United in June 2011, signing a three-year-contract. The former West Ham front man, who scored 7 goals in 13 appearances for the Hammers last season, was Alan Pardew's second signing of the summer, after Yohan Cabaye. One of eight children he has been capped 10 times by Senegal, with three international goals to his name. Ba has also had spells with Rouen, Mouscron and 1899 Hoffenheim.

JOEY BARTON

Born	2 September 1982, Huyton
Debut	22 October 2007 v Tottenham (H)
Previous Club	Manchester City
Appearances/Goals	82/8

Joey joined United in June 2007, playing 23 games that season after an injury hit start to his United career. The attack-minded combative midfielder, with one England cap to his name, made a key contribution to United's Championship success in 2010 and last season was one of the Magpies' outstanding players. With some important goals, some spectacular, and a number of crucial assists, the influential Liverpudlian probably had his best season in a black and white shirt.

LEON BEST

Born	19 September 1986, Nottingham
Debut	5 February 2010 v Cardiff (H)
Previous Club	Coventry City
Appearances/Goals	25/6

Signed from Coventry in the January 2010 transfer window, Leon had already netted nine Championship goals from 15 outings for The Sky Blues in the first part of 2009/10. Injury kept him out until January 2011 but on his full Premier League debut, he hit a terrific hat-trick against West Ham. The pacy frontman, also a republic of Ireland international, started his career at Southampton and will hope to kick-on at St. James' Park in 2011/12.

HATEM BEN ARFA

Born	7 March 1987, Paris
Debut	11 September 2010 v Blackpool (H)
Previous Club	Marseille
Appearances/Goals	4/1

Ben Arfa came to prominence at France's Clairefontaine youth academy. Hatem joined Marseille in 2008 after winning his first full international cap against the Faroe Islands, when he netted the first of two goals to date. Scored a cracker, and United's winner, on his full debut at Everton in September 2010 but suffered a double leg break at Manchester City in October 2010, keeping him sidelined for the rest of the season. In January 2011 he signed a permanent deal with United taking him through the end of the 2014/15 season.

YOHAN CABAYE

Born	14 January 1986, Tourcoing, France
Debut	—
Previous Club	Lille
Appearances/Goals	0/0

Cabaye was United's first 2011 summer signing. The international midfielder played a key role in Lille clinching not only the Lique 1 title – their first championship since 1953/54 – but also the Coupe de France, where they defeated Paris Saint-Germain 1-0 in the final. It was the club's first double since the 1945/46 season and Cabaye's maiden domestic honours. Creative and an excellent passer, Yohan adds to the list of outstanding French talent that has served United well in the past.

FABRICIO COLOCCINI

Born	22 January 1982, Cordoba
Debut	17 August 2008 v Man Utd (A)
Previous Clubs	AC Milan, Deportivo La Coruna
Appearances/Goals	115/4

An outstanding performer last season, and deservedly named United's player of the season. Fabricio joined United from Deportivo La Coruna in 2008 and after taking time to settle and adapt, is now one of the most recognisable faces in the Premier League. He began his career with Argentinos Juniors and made his professional debut in 1998 with Boca Juniors before moving to AC Milan. In 2004 he was an Olympic Gold medallist and he also played in the 2006 World Cup in Germany. Named captain for the 2011/12 season.

SHANE FERGUSON

Born	12 July 1991, Derry, Northern Ireland
Debut	25 August 2010 v Accrington (A)
Previous Club	Academy
Appearances/Goals	9/0

From Derry in Northern Ireland, Shane, skilful and strong, despite his small stature, played his early football at Maiden City. He made his Northern Ireland U21 debut in 2008 against Scotland and won his first full cap coming on as a substitute in Pisa versus Italy on 6 June 2009 (age 17 yrs 329 days) After featuring in the 2010/11 pre-season games, Shane made his full United debut in the League Cup tie at Accrington on 25 August 2010. His Premier League debut came against West Ham on 5 January 2011.

FRASER FORSTER

Born	17 March 1988, Hexham
Debut	—
Previous Clubs	Academy
Appearances/Goals	0/0

Fraser joined the Newcastle United Academy in 2005 from the Royal Grammar School in Newcastle. In 2009/10 he enjoyed a fantastic year out on loan at Norwich City where he helped the Canaries to the League One Championship, last season he excelled with Celtic in the SPL, helping them win the Scottish Cup. Tall and agile, Fraser has turned in some outstanding performances to date away from St.James' Park, but has yet to make his senior United debut.

DAN GOSLING

Born	2 February 1990, Brixham, Devon
Debut	16 January 2011 v Sunderland (A)
Previous Clubs	Plymouth, Everton
Appearances/Goals	1/0

Dan moved to United from Everton in July 2010 signing a four-year contract. The Brixham (Devon) born midfielder had moved to Everton from Plymouth in the January 2008 transfer window having made his debut for the Pilgrims aged just 16. Remembered by Evertonians for his 118th-minute winner in an FA Cup fourth round replay against rivals Liverpool which truly brought his name to the fore, last season was a struggle for Dan as he spent much of it on the sidelines recovering from a cruciate knee ligament injury.

DANNY GUTHRIE

Born	18 April 1987, Shrewsbury
Debut	17 August 2008 v Man Utd (A)
Previous Clubs	Liverpool, Bolton, Southampton
Appearances/Goals	85/7

Danny signed for United in July 2008 from Liverpool, having spent the 2007/08 season on loan at Bolton Wanderers. In 2008/09 he proved what an astute acquisition he had been with a number of solid and consistent displays in the United engine room which gave him the confidence to blossom as United romped to the League title in 2010. A strong running competitive midfielder, the 2010/11 campaign was a bit of a let down in terms of the number of games he played.

JONAS GUTIERREZ

Born	5 July 1983, Buenos Aires, Argentina
Debut	17 August 2008 v Man Utd (A)
Previous Clubs	RCD Mallorca, Velez Sarsfield
Appearances/Goals	113/7

Argentina international Jonas Gutierrez enjoyed a terrific 2010/11 campaign with many outstanding displays down the United flanks. After a barren 2008/09 season in front of goal, his nickname of Spiderman, for wearing the superhero's webbed mask during flamboyant goal celebrations, lit up Tyneside. Previously with Velez Sarsfield in Argentina and Mallorca, Spain his endeavour and enterprise have brought him many admirers. United's only representative at the 2010 World Cup, he missed only one game in United's 2010/11 Premier League campaign.

STEVE HARPER

Born	14 March 1975, Easington
Debut	28 November 1998 v Wimbledon (H)
Previous Clubs	Bradford City (loan), Hartlepool (loan), Huddersfield (loan)
Appearances/Goals	190/0

An integral part of United's success in 2009/10 when he kept a club record 21 clean sheets as United stormed to the Championship title. Very popular on and off the pitch at St. James' Park, the Easington-born shot-stopper is one of the top English goalkeepers in the country. He first broke into the first team during the 1998/99 season and then played in the 1999 FA Cup Final against Manchester United. Possesses terrific reflexes and is a commanding presence in the 18-yard box.

TAMAS KADAR

Born	14 March 1990, Veszprem, Hungary
Debut	26 August 2009 v Huddersfield Town (H)
Previous Clubs	Zalaegerszegi
Appearances/Goals	18/0

Defender Tamas joined United from Hungarian outfit Zalaegerszegi TE for whom he made his debut when only 16. He played 14 times for Zala', scoring once. Comfortable and clever on the ball with a good eye for a pass, Tamas has a great engine too, making him a real 90-minute player. His versatility enables him to play as a full back or central defender. Tamas made 16 solid and assured appearances in his debut season, 2009/10 but has yet to appear in the Premier League for United.

TIM KRUL

Born	3 April 1988, Den Haag, Holland
Debut	2 November 2006 v Palmero (A)
Previous Clubs	Den Haag
Appearances/Goals	34/0

Tim joined United from Dutch side Den Haag in July 2005 and made his debut in the UEFA Cup against Palmero in Sicily in November 2006, turning in a man of the match performance. His league debut came at the Hawthorns on the opening day of the 2009/10 campaign, when he replaced the injured Steve Harper. Last season he made 21 first team appearances and crowned his season by making his full international debut against Brazil in June, keeping a clean sheet.

PETER LOVENKRANDS

Born	29 January 1980, Horsholm, Denmark
Debut	26 August 2008 v Coventry (A)
Previous Club	Schalke 04, Glasgow Rangers
Appearances/Goals	73/26

Peter began his career in his native Denmark with Akademisk Boldklub in 1998, when he was also named Danish U19 Player of the Year. In 2000 he moved to Rangers where he won two SPL titles, as well as one SFA and three League Cups. After a brief spell with Schalke 04 Peter joined United in January 2009. The lively, pacy frontman netted 16 goals as United won the Championship in 2009/10 and last season hit six more, acting as an effective foil to Shola Ameobi and Leon Best.

SYLVAIN MARVEAUX

Born	15 April 1986, Vannes, France
Debut	—
Previous Clubs	Rennes
Appearances/Goals	0/0

Sylvain Marveaux was born in Vannes in the Brittany region of France and joined local club AS Menimur at the age of six. He then joined Vannes OC whilst attending the Pole Espoirs Football de Ploufragan, a smaller regional version of the Clairefontaine academy. He made his Rennes senior debut in the 2006/07 season against Lille when he also earned 11 caps for the France Under-21 team, scoring four goals. Brother Joris plays in the French Ligue 1 for Montpellier.

GABRIEL OBERTAN

Born	26 February 1989, Paris, France
Debut	—
Previous Clubs	Bordeaux, Manchester Utd
Appearances/Goals	0/0

Gabriel joined the Magpies on 8 August 2011 from Manchester United, signing a five-year deal. A former attendee of the famous Clairefontaine academy, he began his career at Bordeaux in France, before joining Manchester United in July 2009. A former member of the France U21 team, he was named as France's best player at the 2009 Toulon Tournament. Gabriel has represented his country at U16 through to U21 level but is still to earn his senior debut. At Old Trafford he made 28 appearances scoring once, against Bursapor in the Champions League.

JAMES PERCH

Born	28 September 1985, Mansfield
Debut	16 August 2010 v Manchester Utd (A)
Previous Clubs	Nottingham Forest
Appearances/Goals	15/0

James signed for United from Nottingham Forest in July 2010, scoring 12 goals in 220 games for the Reds after making his debut as an 18-year-old in 2004. He joined Forest's Academy in 2003 and has shown his versatility by playing across the back-four and in midfield. Last season, his first in the Premier League, he made 15 appearances but was hindered by injuries and some unfortunate yellow cards. A clean start in 2011/12 should see him develop further at United.

NILE RANGER

Born	11 April 1991, London
Debut	8 August 2009 v West Brom (A)
Previous Clubs	Academy
Appearances/Goals	58/3

The London born striker was originally with Southampton but joined United in July 2008 going on to score 22 goals in 43 Reserve and Youth games in 2008/09. Nile won the 'Wor Jackie' award from Sport Newcastle in March 2009 and in four England U19 games in the summer of 2009, scored four goals. His breakthrough in 2009/10 saw him score twice and play a valuable role in the success of the team. Last season he was used mainly from the bench and made a useful impact in many of his appearances.

DANNY SIMPSON

Born	4 January 1987, Manchester
Debut	19 August 2009 v Sheffield Wednesday (A)
Previous Club	Manchester United
Appearances/Goals	72/1

Joined the Magpies on loan in August 2009 from Manchester United, the deal becoming permanent in January 2010. He made the right back position his own, making the third most appearances in the league in 2009/10 (39), behind Steve Harper and Kevin Nolan. He was virtually ever-present last season after recovering from a May 2010 ankle operation. Only one goal to his name, against Peterborough in November 2009, Danny is a solid, dependable and a very popular figure around St. James' Park.

ALAN SMITH

Born	28 October 1980, Rothwell, Leeds
Debut	11 August 2007 v Bolton
Previous Clubs	Leeds Utd, Manchester Utd
Appearances/Goals	92/0

A gritty and determined player every team would wish to have in their ranks. A front man during his time at the United's of Leeds and Manchester, he now fills a holding midfield role with great aplomb. He scored on his Premiership debut for Leeds, when only 18, before moving to Manchester United where he also scored on his debut. Captained the side on over 20 occasions in 2009/10 playing a pivotal role, but injuries limited his involvement last season.

JAMES TAVERNIER

Born	31 October 1991, Bradford
Debut	22 September 2009 v Peterborough (A)
Previous Club	Academy
Appearances/Goals	2/0

Versatile defender able to play full-back or centre-half. Joined United from Walbottle School, which he attended from the age of 15 after moving from West Yorkshire. From the age of 9 he played six seasons with Leeds United before moving to Tyneside. Made his 'first team' bow as a substitute in the 1 – 0 friendly win at Huddersfield on 21 July 2009 and played in the Carling Cup ties at Peterborough and Accrington. Spent time on loan at local Conference side Gateshead last season.

RYAN TAYLOR

Born	19 August 1984, Liverpool
Debut	7 February 2009 v West Brom (A)
Previous Clubs	Tranmere, Wigan
Appearances/Goals	54/6

Ryan Taylor signed for United in February 2009 from Wigan as part of the deal that saw Charles N'Zogbia move in the opposite direction. Ryan began his career at Tranmere before a £750,000 move to Wigan in 2005. Able to fill both the full-back berths, Ryan is a hard tackling defender, comfortable on the ball and with bundles of energy. A great ball-striker, he possesses a deadly free-kick, and also a long throw which makes him a very dangerous opponent. His versatility serves United well.

STEVEN TAYLOR

Born	23 January 1986, Greenwich, London
Debut	25 March 2004 v Real Mallorca (A)
Previous Clubs	Wycombe (loan)
Appearances/Goals	187/13

Steven, a powerful and dominating centre-half, and with a new contract signed and sealed in 2011, was a solid performer for United last season whilst injury permitted. A leader in the best Geordie traditions, his passion and will to win for himself, the team, and the supporters is unbridled – witness his three goals in the final three Premier League games of the 2010/11 campaign. Formerly captain of the England Under 21 team, he has also represented England 'B'. Off the field Steven is the perfect ambassador for United.

CHEIK TIOTE

Born	21 June 1986, Yamoussoukro, Ivory Coast
Debut	18 September 2010 v Everton (A)
Previous Club	FC Twente
Appearances/Goals	28/1

Outstanding last season, Cheik began his career with Ivorian side FC Bibo in his native Yamoussoukro, before being picked up by Anderlecht in 2005. Joining FC Twente in July 2008, he won the Dutch title in 2009/10 under the guidance of Steve McClaren. Tiote appeared in all three of the Ivory Coast's group games at the World Cup in South Africa. Scored his first United goal, a stunning left footed 30 yard volley, to make it 4 – 4 in the dramatic draw with Arsenal at St. James' Park in February 2011 and agreed to a new 6½ year contract later that month.

HARIS VUCKIC

Born	21 August 1992, Ljubljana, Slovenia
Debut	26 August 2009 v Huddersfield Town (H)
Previous Club	MK Domzale
Appearances/Goals	7/0

Promising Slovenian born striker who began his career with NK Domzale. Haris has represented Slovenia at U14, U16 and U17 level and was named Player of the Tournament in the Foca Cup in Bosnia in May 2009, scoring five goals in three games. Made his full United debut at Peterborough on 22 September 2009, but injury has held back his progress since then. Called up to the senior Slovenian squad for the Euro 2012 qualifiers in October 2010 he signed a new 4½ year contract in January 2011.

MIKE WILLIAMSON

Born	8 November 1983, Stoke
Debut	27 January 2010 v Crystal Palace (H)
Previous Club	Portsmouth
Appearances/Goals	48/0

Joined the Magpies in January 2010 from Portsmouth. Stoke born, Williamson started out at Torquay United in 2001 before signing for Southampton. Loan spells back at Torquay, Doncaster and Wycombe followed before a permanent switch to Adams Park in 2005. He joined Watford in 2009 before moving on to Portsmouth. Slotted seamlessly into the United back four for the latter part of the Championship winning campaign and enjoyed an excellent debut year in the Premier League last season.

European nights

European fixtures are very important nights at St. James' Park. There's always a special atmosphere, and in the 120 games United have played (60 of which have been at St. James' Park) there have been many memorable moments.

Newcastle United have played in all of the major European Competitions and in terms of the number of games played, are seventh, in terms of matches played in Europe by English clubs.

Back in 1968, Joe Harvey's side qualified for Europe for the first time and stunned everyone the following year by lifting the Inter Cities Fairs Cup; the forerunner of the UEFA Cup/Europa League. United possessed a solid eleven and Newcastle's tradition of fielding a famous Number 9 at centre-forward continued as big Welshman Wyn Davies was prominent, along with the likes of Bryan "Pop" Robson, Bobby Moncur and Frank Clark.

Back in those days, over 40 years ago, the Fairs Cup, was a very prestigious competition, and a very hard one to win. That was because the European Cup (the Champions League now) only allowed in one team per country, i.e. the League Champions, so teams that finished 2nd, 3rd and 4th in domestic league competitions all played in the Fairs Cup making United's feat in winning the trophy all the more remarkable.

United beat the Hungarians Ujpest Dozsa 6 – 2 over two-legs in the Final. Dozsa were a major force in Europe in the 60s and in the semi-final had defeated the then mighty Leeds United, whilst the Magpies had overcome Glasgow Rangers.

The following year, United lost agonisingly in the quarter finals on the 'away goals' rule to Anderlecht, the killer goal for the Belgium's coming in the final minute at St. James' Park. The Magpies were confident of retaining the trophy and after Keith Dyson made it 3 – 2 with only five minutes left, you could have heard a pin drop in what was one of the most disappointing nights in United's history.

Newcastle made it into the Fairs Cup the following season too, but after putting Italian giants Inter Milan out in the First Round, they meekly surrendered to Pecsi Dozsa, a team without the pedigree of Ujpest, losing horribly 3 – 0 on penalties in

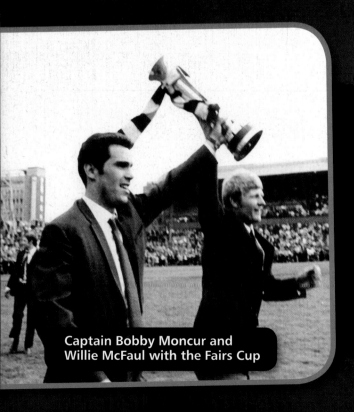

Captain Bobby Moncur and Willie McFaul with the Fairs Cup

Hungary after a 2 – 2 aggregate draw.

There was a seven-year break before European football returned to Gallowgate but United only lasted two rounds in the UEFA Cup, going out to a Johnny Rep inspired Bastia. Rep had been part of the famous Holland team of the 1970s and put on an outstanding display at St. James' Park in the second leg, scoring twice.

After their third place Premier League finish in 1994, United were back in the UEFA Cup once more after a 17-year absence, but after at one stage leading Athletic Bilbao 3 – 0, conspired to go out to the Spaniards on the away goals rule.

United again reached the quarter finals of the UEFA Cup in the 1996/97 season, this time going out to the French side Monaco. United finished second in the Premiership that season and gained qualification into the Champions League after a nail-biting win over Croatia Zagreb in the qualifying round, Temuri Ketsbaia scoring in the last minute of extra time to prevent the tie going to penalties.

United were under-strength for much of their Champions League campaign but after being drawn in a group with Dynamo Kiev, PSV Eindhoven and Barcelona, United did well to finish third in the group, above the mighty Spaniards who were beaten 3 – 2

at St. James' Park in a match that will never be forgotten by those who were present, as Tino Asprilla bagged a fabulous hat-trick.

A brief sojourn into the Cup Winners Cup the following season (now no longer played) came to an abrupt end in Belgrade in Round One whilst their next venture into the UEFA Cup in the 1999/2000 season, ended with defeat to the Italians AS Roma at the third round stage. In 2001/02 United narrowly failed to get into the UEFA Cup once again, losing out in the Final of the Intertoto Cup to French side Troyes.

A fourth place Premiership finish in 2001/02 saw United reach the Qualifying Round of the UEFA Champions League in 2002/03, and after overcoming Zeljeznicar in the Third Qualifying Round, United became the first team in the history of the competition to reach the Second Group Phase after losing their first three games in the First Group Phase. Andy Griffin scored the only goal against Juventus at St. James', Gary Speed and Alan Shearer helped see off Dynamo Kiev, which meant it all went down to the final game in Feyenoord. Leading by two early on, United were pegged back until a sensational ending saw Craig Bellamy grab a 90th minute winner for the black 'n' whites to send the Geordies through to the second group stage. Barcelona and Inter Milan proved too strong for United in the

Andy Griffin nets United's winner against Juventus

next series of games but they did defeat Bayer Leverkusen home and away to finish a respectable third in the group with the stand out game undoubtedly being the 2 – 2 draw in the San Siro against Inter Milan. Alan Shearer put United ahead twice, with over 10,000 Geordies roaring the team on, but Viera and Cordoba ensured it finished all-square.

In 2003/04 Partizan Belgrade knocked United out at the Qualifying stages of the Champions League, which was bitterly disappointing especially as Nobby Solano had given United a 1 – 0 lead after the first leg in Belgrade. It meant the Magpies dropped into the UEFA Cup for the remainder of that season. Successive away wins against Partizan Belgrade, NAC Breda and FC Basel saw United win away in Europe three times on the trot for the first time before agonisingly exiting the competition in Marseille, where Didier Drogba scored twice, at the semi final stage.

The following season United cruised into the Quarter Finals of the UEFA Cup once more, but after taking a 2 goal advantage over Sporting Lisbon in the Quarter Finals, they eventually went down 4 – 2 on aggregate.

The Intertoto Cup brought no joy in 2005/06 but did so in 2006/07, leading to the UEFA Cup again – the last time United enjoyed a

European campaign. Once again United hit the wall in the last-8 of the competition, losing out to Dutch side AZ Alkmaar.

So all in all, a pretty good record for Newcastle United in Europe over the years, one major European title in the trophy cabinet and plenty of thrills and spills along the way – and not too many other clubs can say that!

Red hot in Athens

MISCELLANEOUS RECORDS

Biggest Home Win
Newcastle 5 – 0 NEC Breda
(UEFA Cup 2003/04)

Biggest Away Win
Antwerp 0 – 5 Newcastle
(UEFA Cup 1994/95)

Worst Home Defeat
Newcastle 1 – 4 Inter Milan
(Champions League 2002/03)

Worst Away Defeat
Sporting Lisbon 4 – 1 Newcastle
(UEFA Cup 2004/05)

Highest Home Attendance
59,309, Newcastle v Anderlecht
(Fairs Cup 1969/70)

Lowest Home Attendance
19,046, Newcastle v Bohemiams
(UEFA Cup 1977/78)

Highest Away Attendance
98,000, Dynamo Kiev v Newcastle
(Champions League 1997/98)

Lowest Away Attendance
2,425, Sporting Lokeren v Newcastle
(Intertoto Cup 2001/02)

Successive Victories
5 (1968/69 – 1969/70 Fairs Cup
& 2004/05 UEFA Cup & 2006/07 UEFA Cup)

Successive Defeats
3 (2002/03 Champions League)

Successive Games Scored
19 (2004/5 – 2006/7)

Longest Unbeaten Run
13 (2006/07)

European Appearances

1	Shay Given	1998-2009	62
2	Alan Shearer	1996 2006	49
3	Aaron Hughes	1997 2005	44
4	Nobby Solano	1998-2007	42
5	Shola Ameobi	2000-date	41
6	Gary Speed	1998-2004	39
7	Titus Bramble	2002-2007	39
8	Andy O'Brien	2001-2005	37
9	Laurent Robert	2001-2005	35
10	Olivier Bernard	2000-2005	32

European Goals

1	Alan Shearer	1996-2006	30
2	Shola Ameobi	2000-date	12
3	Craig Bellamy	2001-2005	11
4	Wyn Davies	1966-71	10
5	Bryan Robson	1962-71	9
=	Tino Asprilla	1996-98	9
7	Nobby Solano	1998-2004	7
8	Obafemi Martins	2006-2009	6
9	Jimmy Scott	1967-70	5
=	Gary Speed	1998-2004	5
=	Patrick Kluivert	2004-2005	5
=	Laurent Robert	2001-2005	5

Youngest European Appearance

1 Andrew Carroll
17 yrs 300 days (Palermo, 2/11/06)

2 Aaron Hughes
18 yrs 18 days (Barcelona, 26/11/97)

3 Steven Taylor
18 yrs 61 days (Mallorca, 25/3/04)

4 Tim Krul
18 yrs 213 days (Palermo, 2/11/06)

5 Alan Foggon
18 yrs 249 days (Sporting Lisbon, 30/10/68)

6 James Milner
18 yrs 255 days (Hapoel Sakhnin, 16/9/04)

7 Charles N'Zogbia
18yrs 286 days (Olympiacos, 10/3/05)

Youngest European Scorer

1 Alan Foggon
19 yrs 17 days (Vitoria Setubal, 12/3/69)

2 Charles N'Zogbia
19 yrs 50 days (Dubnica, 17/7/05)

3 James Milner
19 yrs 194 days (Dubnica, 17/7/05)

4 Darren Ambrose
19 yrs 208 days (NAC Breda, 24/9/03)

5 Hugo Viana
19 yrs 255 days (Zeljeznicar, 21/8/02)

6 Shola Ameobi
19 yrs 275 days (Lokeren, 14/7/01)

Overall Record

	Pl	W	D	L	F	A
Home	60	44	8	8	123	47
Away	60	25	14	21	85	72
Total	120	69	22	29	208	119

Season Reviews

2003/04

United's season began in Belgrade in mid-August when the Black-and-Whites beat their Partizan hosts in the first leg of a Champions League Qualifying tie, Nobby Solano hitting the winner. One point from the Premiership games against the Uniteds of Leeds and Manchester didn't appear to be a disastrous prelude to the return leg against the Serbians with the lucrative and prestigious Group Stages of the competition seemingly a mere 90 minutes away. With only Lee Bowyer added to the squad in the close season, United were relying on the team that finished a very good third the previous season.

Against an ordinary Belgrade side, United lost 1–0 on the night in the home leg and 4–3 on penalties – four United players having to hang their heads in shame for missing crucial spot-kicks. To make matters worse, a shell-shocked United lost 2–1 at home to Birmingham three days later while Partizan were looking forward to dream fixtures against Real Madrid and AC Milan. If only.

The 'prize' for losing in the Champions League Qualifiers was to drop down into the UEFA Cup and United made good progress in the early stages of that competition whilst picking up points regularly on the league front. Highlights were the 4–0 hammering of Tottenham at St.James' Park, where Laurent Robert hit two stunning goals, and a 3–0 Gallowgate win over Manchester City. On the down side, United plumbed the depths in the League Cup, losing at home to West Bromwich Albion in October at the first hurdle.

United motored into the New Year in sixth position and then won in fine style, 3–0, at Southampton in Round Three of the FA Cup. The Liverpool juggernaut at Anfield ended any Cup dreams though, in the next round.

Notable Dutch side PSV Eindhoven were beaten in the UEFA Cup Quarter-Finals, which set up a mouth-watering tie with Marseille in the Semi-Finals. The Magpies couldn't break down the French resistance in the goalless first leg on Tyneside and Ivory Coast star striker, Didier Drogba hit United with a double in France to end any hope of a 1969-style European glory season.

Defeated, but not down and out, United fought hard in the remaining three games of the season to gain the necessary points, which would ensure a 5th place finish and with it, more European football the following season. A 1–1 draw at Liverpool on the final day sealed that objective.

Laurent Robert curls in a beauty against Spurs

Season 2003/04

Premiership

Pos	Pld	W	D	L	F	A	Pts
5th	38	13	17	8	52	40	56

FA Cup: R4

League Cup: R3

Uefa: SF

Top scorer: Shearer 28

Avg Attn: 51,966

2004/05

A fifth place finish the previous season under Sir Bobby Robson meant another season of UEFA Cup football for United, who were also aiming for another successful domestic season. Unfortunately things didn't quite pan out as planned.

An outbreak of conjunctivitis in the squad threatened the opening day's fixture at Middlesbrough, but it went ahead and United came away with a point when it should really have been three, Jimmy Floyd Hasselbaink netting a controversial last-minute equaliser for Boro. After failing to register a win in the next three games, the last being a 4–2 reverse at Aston Villa, United took the decision to part company with Sir Bobby ending a five-year reign at Gallowgate for the former England boss.

Coach John Carver took charge for the visit of Blackburn the following weekend, and United eased to a convincing 3–0 victory. However, he was just keeping the seat warm for Graeme Souness, the latest man to take on one of the toughest, but best jobs in football. Souness joined from Blackburn Rovers and was United's fifth different manager in the past eight years.

Souness made an impressive start, a nine-match unbeaten run seeing The Magpies rise to 7th in the Premiership whilst at the same time, progress was being made in the UEFA

David James foils United's Craig Bellamy

Cup. That was as high as United climbed in the League, though, as frustratingly inconsistent form left the side languishing just below mid-table for the rest of the season, that despite seasoned international players Patrick Kluivert, Nicky Butt and Stephen Carr being amongst those who had joined the Club before the start of the season. A 12-match unbeaten run throughout February and March couldn't hide United's shortcomings, but to be fair success was hinted at in the FA and UEFA Cups.

Chelsea had ended United's interest in the League Cup back in November whilst two favourable draws in the FA Cup had seen United reach the Fifth Round. Excellent wins over Chelsea and Tottenham took United through to a semi-final against Manchester United in Cardiff whilst at the same time Sporting Lisbon were set to provide the opposition in the UEFA Cup Quarter-Final. A horror four days was to follow. Despite at one stage leading the Portuguese side 2–0 on aggregate, United crumbled and lost 4–2 on aggregate and then followed that with a weary, hollow display against Sir Alex Ferguson's side – the 4–1 scoreline not flattering the Reds one bit. A long campaign finished on a low-key note with seven Premiership games being crammed into the final 25 days of the season.

Season 2004/05

Premiership

Pos	Pld	W	D	L	F	A	Pts
14th	38	10	14	14	47	57	44

FA Cup: SF

League Cup: R4

Uefa: QF

Top scorer: Shearer 19

Avg Attn: 51,844

spot the difference

Can you spot 6 differences between the pictures below?

crossword

Clues Down

1 Nigerian International left-back
2 Keeper from the mld 90s
3 French flair winger
4 Striker signed from Wimbledon
5 'Quick' striker
6 On loan French striker, late 90s
7 Brazilian defender
8 2010/11 Skipper
9 Chilean international

Clues Across

1 French defender
2 Lifted Carling Cup in 2011
3 Our Argentine Olympian
4 Scored his last United goal at Sunderland
5 Hit 41 goals in one season
6 Cup winning captain in 1932
7 Former striker now at Ipswich

Answers on page 60

where are they now?

Have you ever wondered what the former players of Newcastle United are doing with their lives? Here's a selection from the recent past and what they're up to now.

Scott Sellars

Left Midfielder
1993-1995
75 apps, 8 goals

After joining Bolton Wanderers in 1995 Sellars, a cultured left sided midfielder, moved to Huddersfield Town in 1999 before moving to Danish side AGF Aarhus. He later went on to sign for Mansfield Town in March 2002, before becoming involved in coaching and working with the youngsters coming into the club. Today, he coaches Manchester City's Under 18 team.

Barry Venison

Defender 1992-1995
133 apps, 1 goal

After leaving Newcastle in 1995, Barry, who captained United with great authority, moved to Galatasaray in Turkey and then to Southampton before retiring with a back injury. He then took up punditry for Sky Sports before moving to ITV. In 2000 he launched an on-line sports memorabilia auction site called 'bid4sport.com' which aimed to raise money for charity. In 2001 he made an appearance in the comedy film Mike Bassett: England Manager where he starred as himself. Now in property development in California.

Andy Cole

Striker 1993-1995
84 apps, 68 goals

After Cole left Newcastle he went on to play for another six teams, before finally retiring from football after a 19 year long career in 2008. In August 2009, Cole worked with MK Dons before going on to coach the forwards at Huddersfield Town. He then went back to Manchester United in 2010 where he works at the Carrington Training Ground whilst completing his coaching badges. A real fan favourite for his goals at St. James' Park.

Robbie Elliott

Left Back 1989-1997, 2001-2006
188 apps, 12 goals

After leaving Newcastle in 1997, Robbie, an assured full-back, returned in 2001 to play intermittently for the club before finally being released in 2006. In the summer of 2008, Elliott came back to United and was named as the new assistant Fitness and Conditioning coach. Robbie then went on to work with Nike's SPARQ team where he focused on helping athletes improve their sports performance, and also joined the USA Soccer's strength and conditioning team.

Kevin Gallacher

Striker 1999-2001
47 apps, 6 goals

Brought to Newcastle by Sir Bobby Robson, Gallacher, a clever and sprightly forward, had two years on Tyneside before retiring in 2002. He now works as a co-commentator and studio analyst for BBC Radio 5 Live, Sky Sports, Setanta, BBC Scotland and Channel 5 and is also a columnist in the Lancashire Telegraph. In 2010, Kevin began working for ITV sport on their coverage of the FA Cup.

Steve Howey

Defender 1989-2000
242 apps, 7 goals

Cool, calm and very comfortable on the ball, Steve played for Manchester City, Leicester City, Bolton Wanderers and Hartlepool United after leaving Newcastle. He completed a short spell as a Youth Team Coach at Middlesbrough before making a playing return with Bishop Auckland. In 2007, Howey went on to become a coach at East Durham College Football Development Centre before becoming Head Coach in 2010.

Alan Neilson

Defender 1991-1995
50 apps, 1 goal

Welsh international Alan transferred from Newcastle to Southampton in June 1995 and after playing for a number of different teams became coach at Luton and Barnfield College. Just before retiring, he played out a short-term contract for Salisbury City and in June 2008, Neilson joined Luton Town as Youth Development Coach. Whilst at Luton Town he was given the position of first-team coach, and today is the First Team Development Manager.

Liam O'Brien

Midfielder
1988-1994
185 apps, 22 goals

Irishman O'Brien, famous for his stunning free kick at Roker Park in October 1992, played a major role in Newcastle winning the First Division title that season. He then made a move to Tranmere Rovers and then Cork City before finally joining Bohemians in 2000 as a player coach. After retiring, O'Brien went on to be assistant manager at Shamrock Rovers and is now assistant manager at Bohemians.

Niki Papavasiliou

Midfielder 1993-1994
7 apps

After one season at Newcastle, Papavasiliou, a neat and tidy midfielder, went on to play for OFI Crete and others as well as playing 38 times for his National Team. Once retired from Football, Niki went on to manage teams such as Olympiakos Nicosia, OFI Crete, Doxa Katakopia, and now manages Enosis Neon Paralimni FC in Cyprus.

Tino Asprilla

Striker 1996-1998
63 apps, 18 goals

After leaving Newcastle in 1998, Tino, one of United's most flamboyant goalscorers, rejoined Parma before having brief spells with six other South American sides. In July 2009, Asprilla, who won 57 international caps, officially stopped playing and had a retirement match in Colombia. He is currently running an academy, coaching young players in Colombia and is still a frequent visitor to Tyneside.

Olivier Bernard

Defender 2000-2005
145 apps, 6 goals

After being part of Sir Bobby Robson's side, attacking full-back Olivier left Newcastle and went to play for Southampton and Rangers before returning to Newcastle for a short spell. After retiring in 2008 due to a hip injury, Bernard became involved with the Show Racism the Red Card organisation which helps educate people, particularly children in the North East, on this subject.

Paul Bracewell

Midfield 1992-1995
87 apps, 4 goals

After leaving Newcastle in 1995, and having another spell at Sunderland, Paul, a hugely competitive and effective midfielder, took on a player/coach role with Fulham where he later became manager. He then moved on to become manager of Halifax Town before starting up his own soccer complex called Complete Football. Situated in Gosforth Park, Newcastle, he remains there today.

former players

Draw a line to match each current player's former club

Peter Lovenkrands	Liverpool
Steve Harper	Manchester United
Ryan Taylor	Real Mallorca
Cheik Tiote	Everton
Danny Simpson	Schalke 04
Jonas Gutierrez	Seaham Red Star
Danny Guthrie	Wigan Athletic
Dan Gosling	FC Twente

And the same for these former stars

David Ginola	Everton
Alan Shearer	Parma
Rob Lee	Marseille
Gary Speed	Boca Juniors
Tino Asprilla	Blackburn Rovers
Habib Beye	Charlton Athletic
Emre	Paris St Germain
Nobby Solano	Inter Milan

Answers on page 60

wordsearch

See if you can find 25 Newcastle players, all from overseas, from the Premier League era.

E	W	E	B	A	S	S	E	D	A	S	D	H	J	L	K	W
R	A	R	E	V	E	A	Q	B	Z	O	F	G	H	G	H	A
T	S	Y	V	C	R	S	W	E	X	L	U	Q	U	E	D	K
Y	A	L	O	N	I	G	E	Y	C	A	G	F	I	F	R	S
F	D	T	B	X	T	X	R	E	V	N	H	S	G	U	S	D
C	F	B	E	R	N	A	R	D	B	O	S	D	L	D	K	F
O	G	Y	O	C	S	I	X	S	N	O	J	S	F	S	L	G
R	A	U	P	L	Y	C	T	A	R	S	K	A	D	W	U	M
D	L	K	I	A	U	R	E	G	I	T	T	O	H	E	I	A
O	L	J	S	N	K	V	Y	Q	M	D	L	E	S	R	V	I
N	I	H	T	H	J	A	S	A	Z	I	B	A	D	T	E	A
E	R	G	O	E	H	K	U	W	R	O	B	E	R	T	R	B
U	P	F	N	Z	G	U	I	E	H	D	I	R	M	Y	T	S
I	S	D	E	O	F	D	J	D	I	S	T	I	N	R	S	T
O	A	A	N	R	E	I	U	R	N	N	A	M	A	H	E	E
L	H	S	M	X	W	V	Y	T	G	F	U	T	W	U	D	K
M	N	O	N	I	L	E	C	R	A	M	Y	Y	E	O	A	G

ASPRILLA	**BASSEDAS**	**BERNARD**
BEYE	**CORDONE**	**DABIZAS**
DISTIN	**EMRE**	**FAYE**
GINOLA	**HAMANN**	**HOTTIGER**
KETSBAIA	**KLUIVERT**	**KRUL**
LUQUE	**MARCELINO**	**PISTONE**
ROBERT	**ROSSI**	**ROZEHNAL**
SOLANO	**VIDUKA**	**XISCO**

Answers on page 60

Newcastle United Foundation

Newcastle United Foundation is the official charity of Newcastle United Football Club.

It aims to use the local passion for football to encourage learning and promote healthy lifestyles that will make a real difference to the lives of children, young people and families in our region.

Whilst the players consolidated their position in the Premier League in 2010/11, the team at Newcastle United Foundation had a fantastic year of activities out in the community. The Foundation continued to provide opportunities for young people to play football through its grassroots coaching and schools skills programmes and in addition has created a range of educational projects to inspire learning and promote healthy lifestyles, reaching over 10,000 individuals.

Alan Pardew Backs New Grass Roots Coaching Programme

Manager Alan Pardew lent his support to a new initiative which promotes coaching excellence across the region.

The new scheme, called "Coach the Coach", is being led by Newcastle United Foundation A License coaches Neil Winskill and Ben Dawson. The specialist coaching clinics are designed to support football coaches working at grassroots level in the local community.

The objective is to provide practical support to both paid and volunteer coaches to support the development of talented young players from this region.

Enterprise

Shefki Kuqi visited Armstrong School, Excelsior Academy in Scotswood to help students with a mock enterprise challenge to design and market a new strip for the Club.

The player chatted with the students and then picked out his favourite designs.

Finland international striker Kuqi said: "It has been really nice to come along and see what the children have been up to. I'm leaving

here with a new shirt designed by two lads which I think is great."

The activity was part of Newcastle United Foundation's Enterprise Academy, which aims to stimulate young minds about business and raise their aspirations to stay in employment.

Match fit families

Dan Gosling and Peter Beardsley visited St John's Primary School in Benwell, Newcastle in January to meet a group of families aiming to become Match Fit.

The duo were attending the launch of Newcastle United Foundation's new Match Fit Families Initiative. They joined parents and children from the school in a session about becoming fit and healthy families. The session included a fun, interactive "Play Your Sugars and Fats Right" nutrition game.

Leon Best and Mike Williamson Visit Soccer School

Leon Best and Mike Williamson went back to soccer school to meet the stars of the future at Complete Football, Gosforth in February.

The players were attending Newcastle United Foundation's Half Term Soccer School where they took part in an interactive training session.

Newcastle United Foundation runs football coaching camps in every school holiday plus Saturday skills Centres every Saturday in term time for girls and boys of all abilities. A must for any budding young NUFC fan.

During the six weeks families learn about the Eatwell Plate, Foods for Fuel, Fruit & Vegetables, Heart Health, Drinks and hydration and how to cook nutritious, affordable meals for the whole family.

On the spot

Twelve-year-old Chris McKitten, who lost his leg to cancer, scored a penalty in front of a packed Gallowgate End at the Wolves game.

Chris attends the Foundation's coaching centre at Gateshead Stadium every week and has been selected to play for the FA Centre of Excellence. He is also a season ticket holder, coming along to every home game with his Grandad.

Newcastle United Foundation's Disability Football scheme is funded by BBC Children in Need. The programme involves school coaching sessions, after school clubs, satellite coaching camps and fixtures across Newcastle, Gateshead, North Tyneside and Northumberland.

past and present quiz

See how much you know about Newcastle United past and present!

1 In which year did Newcastle United last play at Wembley?

2 Who was Newcastle's first Premier League win against in 1993?

3 Tony Green, Micky Burns and Keith Dyson all have connections with which other team?

4 Who did United beat when they won the FA Cup for the first time in 1910?

5 Jackie Milburn, Bobby Cowell and which other United player won three FA Cup winners medals in the 1950s?

6 Which British team did United beat on the way to winning the European Fairs Cup in 1969?

7 Which country did 90s centre half Philippe Albert play for?

8 Which French team did Chris Waddle play for?

9 Who did United beat 8 – 0 in 1999, a club record in the Premier League?

10 Who is the only Peruvian to play for United?

Answers on page 60

TOP 10 GOALS 2010/11

It was a cracking season for goals once again, especially on Tyneside with United being the second highest home goal scorers in the Premier League, behind Champions Manchester United. It wasn't easy to select only 10, but here they are, including ten different scorers too, and listed in the order they were scored throughout the season.

Joey Barton
v Aston Villa H, 22/08/10

The first of six goals that flew past Villa's Brad Friedel on a memorable afternoon at St. James' Park. Only 12 minutes were on the clock when Joey Barton unleashed a right-foot pile driver from some 25 yards, that swerved and dipped its way past Friedel into the top of the Leazes End net. Joey would score a similar strike at Stevenage in the FA Cup but this was the one that crucially opened up Villa.

Hatem Ben Arfa
v Everton A, 18/9/10

On his full Newcastle debut, French international Hatem Ben Arfa gave United fans a taste of what he's capable of. Hitting the only goal of the game, Hatem picked the ball up 25 yards out and struck an exocet missile-like left foot shot that two keepers wouldn't have got near, let alone Tim Howard in the Gwladys Street End goal. Sadly, his season was to be ended by injury two weeks later at Manchester City.

Ryan Taylor
v Accrington Stanley A, 25/8/10

United faced a tricky Carling Cup tie at the Crown Ground but were boosted by a trademark Ryan Taylor strike after 36 minutes. Well renowned for his dead ball ability, Ryan picked up a Donaldson pass just over the half way line, strode forward and before the home defenders could close him down, let fly from fully 30-yards. The result was an arrow like strike that left keeper Dunbavin grasping at thin air.

Kevin Nolan
v Sunderland H, 31/10/10

Midway through the first half, United were looking for the breakthrough and Kevin Nolan was the man who got it. Joey Barton's corner was headed down by Mike Williamson and the skipper was the first to react to acrobatically spin and hit an overhead kick past Mignolet and his defenders on the line – a wonderful piece of improvisation and skill. The rest is history as the skipper grabbed two more goals to complete a glorious hat-trick.

Shola Ameobi
v Sunderland H, 31/10/10

Shola had already netted from the penalty spot but this goal was something extra special. Barton played in Simpson down the right, his cross was smacked against the crossbar by Andy Carroll's forehead and when the rebound came out, Shola was there to athletically pounce and volley home, hip height, an unstoppable right-footed volley – his sixth strike against the old enemy and one to savour.

Andy Carroll
v Liverpool H, 18/12/10

Alan Pardew's first game in charge, United hanging on to three points as the clock ticked down, step forward Andy Carroll to thunder one past Pepe Reina to seal the points. It was a truly majestic strike, thumped home with immense power from 25 yards at the Gallowgate End as the Reds' defence simply stood back and watched – a goal from the moment it left his foot.

Fabricio Coloccini
v Tottenham H, 22/1/11

This was an end-to-end affair and it took a goal from an unusual source to break the deadlock. On the hour mark, Danny Guthrie swung over a deep cross to the left hand side of the Spurs box, Fabricio Coloccini chested it down and showing all the skill of a genuine frontman, stepped inside Alan Hutton to shoot past Carlo Cudicini into the Gallowgate End net. Sadly Aaron Lennon's late strike prevented it being a glorious winner.

TOP 10 GOALS
2010/11

Peter Lovenkrands
v Wolves H, 2/4/11

This was a terrific team goal. Firstly Fabricio Coloccini showed great skill and dexterity down the right, the Argentine then played a slide rule pass to Joey Barton on the right wing who crossed low for Peter Lovenkrands to slot past Wayne Hennessey from 8 yards out. Simple, fast flowing football at its best.

Cheik Tiote
v Arsenal H, 5/2/11

Perhaps the most memorable goal of the season, both for its quality and significance, and a hugely popular goalscorer too. 3 – 4 down with only three minutes left, when Joey Barton's free kick was headed out, Tiote hit the sweetest of left foot volleys past a despairing Wojciech Szczesny to level things up. He then set off on a wild celebratory run back towards the Leazes End, collapsing onto the turf before eventually emerging from a sea of black and white shirts that had piled on top of him.

Jonas Gutierrez
v Wolves H, 2/4/11

United were cruising as the game entered injury time. Wolves won a corner and when it was cleared, Steven Taylor emerged with the ball, charging down the left wing. Passing the half way line he fed Jonas Gutierrez, who, rather than head to the corner flag to waste time, cut inside to curl a delightful right footed strike low into Hennessey's left hand corner – an exquisite finish.

Steven Taylor's dream team

Steven Taylor is one of United's longest serving players, a fine central defender, local boy made good and a player totally dedicated to bringing success to Newcastle United.

During his time at Gallowgate he has played with and seen at close quarters some of the very best players who have graced the St. James' Park turf.

Here Steven has enjoyed selecting his best players, an XI he'd be very proud to manage! Read on and you'll find out why.

Pavel Srnicek
Goalkeeper

Pavel was a real extrovert but more than that, he was a very capable goalkeeper who played a crucial role in re-establishing the club in the Premier League in the mid 1990s, just when I was enjoying watching the team as a young lad. I used to love the multi-coloured shirts he wore too, and when he came out with the ball and sold a dummy to an on-rushing attacker, it brought the house down at St. James' Park. Pavel will always be a Geordie in my book.

Steve Watson
Right Back

Like me, Steve was a local lad and must have been thrilled to play in front of the Newcastle public. He was a great athlete too and by far the best option for this position as he could get up and down the pitch all day, such was his level of fitness. He was versatile as well, capable of playing in the middle of the park, but I think right-back was where he performed best. He could finish too, cool in front of goal, and did you see that famous flip throw in too? Magic!

Jonathan Woodgate
Centre Half

Woody was a real class act, and a great lad off the field too. He filled the centre half role with great aplomb, was good in the air, very able on the ground, but his best asset was that he was a tremendous reader of the game. I also viewed Woody as a terrific leader too, he was composed and could bring the ball out of the back-four with ease. I've rarely seen a player so comfortable in his position and but for injury, he could have won many more England caps than he did.

Stuart Pearce
Left Back

I remember Stuart playing for England more than anything else and was hugely impressed by his devotion to the cause, hard as nails, but solid, reliable and what a great shot he had on him too. So I was very pleased to see him come to Newcastle even though it was towards the end of his career. I'm sure he was the ultimate professional as that was the impression he always gave and just by watching him from the terraces, you could learn an awful lot about the art of defending.

Philippe Albert
Centre Half

A fantastic footballer who rarely gave the ball away, and when he came upfield with the ball, he was awesome. Philippe was one of my favourite players, he exuded class and must have been a dream to play alongside. He had a great ability to pick out a player with his trusty left foot and covered a lot of ground without any real pace. Unfortunately he suffered from injuries during his time here but of course left one abiding memory for everyone – his chip over Peter Schmeichel in the 5-0.

Rob Lee
Centre Midfield

Rob had a fantastic 10-year career at St. James' Park. From what I remember he began as a wide-man but switched to the centre with great effect. Had a terrific work-rate and a real goal threat going forward. Two footed, Rob served the club superbly, in which time he deservedly went to the World Cup with England in 1998. And I was at Wembley as a fan for the FA Cup Semi Final in 2000 against Chelsea and although we lost, his goal there really was something special.

Alan Shearer
Centre Forward

What more can you say about the 'Big Man' that hasn't already been said? Everyone knows his goalscoring record and I have to say he was a phenomenal player, so hungry for goals but aside from that, a top professional who liked nothing better than seeing Newcastle United win, with him scoring too of course. Fantastically strong, it was almost impossible to get the ball off him in training before he'd 'burst the net' more often than not.

David Ginola
Left Wing

David was unplayable in his day. I'm told in training he had so much skill on the ball his teammates, who were all class players as well, just had to stand back and admire him. He could beat defenders left or right and scored some great goals too, I particularly recall a left foot volley against Ferencvaros in the UEFA Cup that was truly stunning. In his first season he was absolutely awesome and I just wish he could have stayed on Tyneside a little longer.

Craig Bellamy

The Welsh wizard as some called him. He had pace to burn and would scare defenders to death.

I certainly found that in training! Bellers was a great finisher too and scored some terrific goals for us. Sadly, like Kieron Dyer, with whom he played so well with, he suffered a bit with injury during his time here. Like Joey Barton, he has an incredible knowledge of all things football, for example, he knows the names of all the top players all over the world, who they played for and what sort of players they were.

Tino Asprilla
Centre Forward

You have to say Tino was unique. Some people say he didn't fit into the team but I don't buy that. From the moment he arrived he set Tyneside alight and the fans absolutely loved him. He made an immediate impact in his first game, then remember his superb goal in the 4-3 game at Liverpool when he flicked it in with the outside of his right foot like no one else could do. And then there was his Barcelona hat-trick which was one of the most sensational nights I've ever witnessed.

Gary Speed
Centre Midfield

A credit to his profession, I'm delighted to see him doing so well in management at the moment. Often under-rated, but never in my view, he was the 'go-to' player when you needed help. He never hid, would help you out all the time and never stopped encouraging. He was fabulous in the air and had a real presence on the pitch. He was also as strong a player as you could see and never shirked a challenge. Stronger on his left side, but a hugely gifted player too. A consummate professional off the field as well.

So here is the full Steven Taylor team

Name	Country	Apps/Goals
Pavel Srnicek	Czech Rep	190/0
Steve Watson	England	263/14
Stuart Pearce	England	52/1
Jonathan Woodgate	England	37/0
Philippe Albert	Belgium	138/12
Rob Lee	England	381/56
Gary Speed	Wales	285/40
David Ginola	France	75/7
Craig Bellamy	Wales	128/42
Alan Shearer	England	406/206
Tino Asprilla	Columbia	63/18
Manager		Steven Taylor

spot the ball

Can you guess which ball is in the correct spot?

Answers on page 60

57

Player Spotlight
Yohan Cabaye

Yohan Cabaye was born on January 14, 1986, in Tourcoing – a city in northern France just outside Lille. His father, Didier, was a former footballer with Lens and spent a year there at the age of 16 before suffering a double leg fracture, which ended his career.

Cabaye Senior went on to play for amateur clubs Stade Jean-Macé and US Tourcoing, which later merged to form Tourcoing FC.

Yohan played for hometown club Tourcoing FC at the age of five, and after seven years in their youth academy joined Lille. He progressed through the ranks at Lille and six years after arriving at the club made his professional debut in the 2004/05 season.

That campaign also coincided with Lille winning the Intertoto Cup. A creative midfielder, Cabaye has represented France at under 16, under 18, under 19, under 20, and under 21 level, wearing the captain's armband for the latter. He helped the under 19s to the 2005 European Under 19 Football Championship, before representing the under 20s at the Toulon Tournament the following year.

Cabaye was called up to the French senior team for the first time under new manager Laurent Blanc and made his international debut in August 2010 in a friendly against Norway. He was called back into the squad in September for Les Bleus' European Championships qualification matches against Belarus and Bosnia and Herzegovina, but withdrew because of injury. He won his fourth international cap in June 2011, the day before he signed for United as France beat Poland 1-0 in Warsaw.

In 2010/11 Cabaye played a key role in Lille clinching not only the Lique 1 title – their first championship since 1953/54 – but also the Coupe de France, where they defeated Paris Saint-Germain 1-0 in the final. It was the club's first double since the 1945/46 season and Cabaye's maiden domestic honours.

Yohan is a box-to-box midfielder and a player with great vision, superb ball control and excellent technical ability. He is the latest in a line of top quality French players to join United in the Premier League era, 15 others having already worn the black 'n' white shirt since 1993, including the likes of David Ginola, Laurent Robert and more recently, Hatem Ben Arfa.

Talking after he signed about the 2011/12 campaign, Yohan said:

"I'm really happy to be at Newcastle United. I've just seen the facilities and the magnificent stadium. The people are very welcoming so it's really great to be here. I want to adapt to the rhythm here, which is a lot quicker than in France, and it is one of the best leagues in the world.

"I like being on the ball, playing with the ball and making lots of passes. I am not a big dribbler, but I like unsettling the opposition with short or long passes. I like going for goal, but I am also a player who knows how to defend and make lots of effort to get the ball back.

"I am really excited about discovering the Premier League, St. James' Park and all of Newcastle's fans, and hopefully this season will go as well as possible for the team and for me. I am really excited to wear this new shirt."

Fact File

Born	14 January 1986, Tourcoing, Lille
Age	25
Height	5'9" (1.75m)
Weight	12st
Position	Midfield
Squad No.	4
Date Signed	10 June 2011
Previous Club	Lille
International Career	4 France caps, 2010-date

quiz answers

Season Quiz 2010/11 (page 27)
1. Andy Carroll and Shola Ameobi (v Man City and Wigan)
2. Stevenage
3. Andy Carroll (v Aston Villa)
4. FC Twente
5. Accrington Stanley
6. Fulham and Manchester United
7. West Ham and Birmingham
8. Brazil
9. Two
10. Sunderland

Wordsearch (page 47)

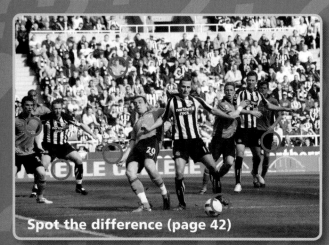

Spot the difference (page 42)

Past and Present (page 50)
1. 2000 (FA Cup Semi Final v Chelsea)
2. Everton
3. Blackpool
4. Barnsley
5. Bobby Mitchell
6. Glasgow Rangers
7. Belgium
8. Marseille
9. Sheffield Wednesday
10. Nobby Solano

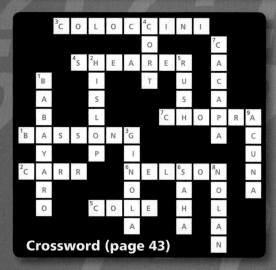

Crossword (page 43)

Spot the ball (page 57)

Former clubs (page 46)
Peter Lovenkrands	Schalke 04
Steve Harper	Seaham Red Star
Ryan Taylor	Wigan Athletic
Cheik Tiote	FC Twente
Danny Simpson	Manchester United
Jonas Gutierrez	Real Mallorca
Danny Guthrie	Liverpool
Dan Gosling	Everton

Former stars (page 46)
David Ginola	Paris St Germain
Alan Shearer	Blackburn Rovers
Rob Lee	Charlton Athletic
Gary Speed	Everton
Tino Asprilla	Parma
Habib Beye	Marseille
Emre	Inter Milan
Nobby Solano	Boca Juniors

2011/12 Barclays Premier League Fixtures

Date	Opposition	H/A	K-Off	Score
Sat 13 August	Arsenal	H	5.30	
Sat 20 August	Sunderland	A	12.00	
Sun 28 August	Fulham	H	1.00	
Mon 12 September	Queens Park Rangers	A	8.00	
Sat 17 September	Aston Villa	A	3.00	
Sat 24 September	Blackburn Rovers	H	3.00	
Sat 1 October	Wolverhampton W	A	3.00	
Sun 16 October	Tottenham Hotspur	H	4.00	
Sat 22 October	Wigan Athletic	H	3.00	
Mon 31 October	Stoke City	A	8.00	
Sat 5 November	Everton	H	12.45	
Sat 19 November	Manchester City	A	3.00	
Sat 26 November	Manchester United	A	3.00	
Sat 3 December	Chelsea	H	3.00	
Sat 10 December	Norwich City	A	3.00	
Sat 17 December	Swansea City	H	3.00	
Wed 21 December	West Brom	H	7.45	
Mon 26 December	Bolton Wanderers	A	3.00	
Sat 31 December	Liverpool	A	12.45	
Mon 2 January	Manchester United	H	3.00	
Sat 14 January	Queens Park Rangers	H	3.00	
Sat 21 January	Fulham	A	3.00	
Wed1 February	Blackburn Rovers	A	8.00	
Sat 4 February	Aston Villa	H	3.00	
Sat 11 February	Tottenham Hotspur	A	3.00	
Sat 25 February	Wolverhampton W	H	3.00	
Sat 3 March	Sunderland	H	3.00	
Sat 10 March	Arsenal	A	3.00	
Sat 17 March	Norwich City	H	3.00	
Sat 24 March	West Brom	A	3.00	
Sat 31 March	Liverpool	H	3.00	
Sat 7 April	Swansea City	A	3.00	
Mon 9 April	Bolton Wanderers	H	3.00	
Sat 14 April	Chelsea	A	3.00	
Sat 21 April	Stoke City	H	3.00	
Sat 28 April	Wigan Athletic	A	3.00	
Sat 5 May	Manchester City	H	3.00	
Sun 13 May	Everton	A	4.00	

Where's Monty?